# 67

## CONVERSATIONS
## TO HAVE WITH YOURSELF
*That Will Change Your Life*
By Edward J. Peters

# COPYRIGHT

Publisher

PETERSCOMMUNICATIONS
1555 Berenda Place
El Cajon, CA 92020

## DEDICATION

*I dedicate this book to my dear wife Dorothy and our six wonderful children,*
*Laura, Nick, Joan, Sue, David and Carol, along with their families,*
*who have inspired me to give new life to the thoughts,*
*ideas and conversations that gave us the guidance*
*to live the life we were meant to live*
*with the blessings of*
*The One up above.*

## PREFACE

*There is something very powerful
about having positive, personal conversations
that will change your life.*

*We talk to ourselves constantly.
We say things to ourselves we would never say to another.
What we say and how we say it affects how we feel,
how we act and especially how we feel about our lives.
That is the special power vested in each of us.*

*If we could control what we say to ourselves,
we would have absolute control of our future.
The level of success we would experience internally –
the happiness, joy, ecstasy, love, or anything else we desire –
is the direct result of the depth of conversations we have with ourselves.*

*Controlling what we say to ourselves gives us total control
of our confidence as well as our potential achievements.
We are then in complete control of how we feel, how we interpret,
how we allow it to affect our mood, our actions and our life.
In the end, nothing has meaning except the meaning we give it.*

*Controlling our internal conversation is the launch-pad for happiness.
Success is about the positive conversations we have with ourselves.
It's all about what we continually program into our mind.
They are the most important conversations we can have,
for it determines what we do, how well we do it
and why we do it.*

*What we achieve in life is determined by
how successful we communicate with ourselves.
The greatest gift of successful people
is their ability to take positive action.
Continuous, positive, internal communication
is the source of their power.*

*That is why we created "67 Conversations to Have with Yourself".*
*These stimulating conversations are designed to accomplish two things.*
*1. Stop internal negative dialogue and replace it*
*with something more positive.*
*2. Expand internal conversations to those*
*that will help change your life.*
*They could also be shared*
*with your family*
*and become the setting for*
*communicating strong family values.*
*They could become an important teaching moment.*
*All topics have been designed to be brief, concise and give you*
*the ability to expand conversations defining a transformative way to*
*think about every aspect of your life.*

*All are designed to crystalize life-changing opportunities.*
*Each subject is dedicated to expanding your life with a way to think and act.*
*They are highly memorable, thought provoking,*
*self-stimulating and self-motivating.*

*They will initiate deeper thoughts about how you live, culminating in personal*
*actions that motivate a direct and immediate change in your life.*
*These are important conversations you can have with yourself and your family.*

*This book is the culmination of our most inspirational teachings, conversations,*
*thoughts and quotes created and shared over the years. Their longevity, their*
*proven motivational power and their continued success*
*leads us to believe they should now be shared.*

*Something positive to think about - Something interesting to talk about –*
*Something motivating to act upon – Something life-changing to do.*
*So, here's to having something important to say to yourself,*
*that will change your life.*
*Enjoy!*

# INTRODUCTION

This book of thoughts, ideas, discussions and
conversations are organized into 67 separate motivational subjects.
They are designed to act as stimulators for a deeper, more
thoughtful conversation with yourself
and potentially with your family or friends.

This book covers innovative ideas and
proven methods to achieve success, improve life,
increase sales ability, expand internal as well as
external communication techniques,
improve decision making techniques,
and build self-confidence along with
many, many more life changing concepts.
Each of the 67 topics are numbered in a specific sequence.
Plan to concentrate on only one subject or conversation at a time.
The time you devote to each conversation should also be used
to engage in a deep self-examination as to the meaning,
the exploration, the determination and finally
the action suggested designed to deliver
a positive, life-changing result.
It acts as a call to action.

Additional readings
will open a deeper and expanded variation of the same theme.
You will develop a more comprehensive understanding as well as
incorporating a unique method to assimilate new ideas
into your thinking and your life.

Take sufficient time to fully develop a single idea
until it becomes part of who you are and
especially who you desire to become.
When you engage these conversations
with your family, they could
become a "teaching moment"
on family values, aspirations,
conduct, actions and accountability.

*To gain immediate and lasting results from this book and
receive the maximum impact from these conversations,
we highly recommend the following:*

*After reading each conversation, ask yourself the following questions.*

*What is the meaning of this conversation?
How can I apply this to my daily life?
How can I do it successfully?
What is the action being called for?
What actions will I take?
How can I apply this to my family?*

*Document your answers in a separate file or pad to keep as a reference. Review
your entries for each conversation throughout the week. Add additional notes
and thoughts regarding each subject until you feel you have explored the full
potential for that conversation's ability
to change your life.*

*Have very stimulating life-changing conversations
with the most important person in your life.
You!*

# CONTENT

# THOUGHTS & ACTIONS

*Gain lasting results from this conversation by asking yourself the following questions and noting your answers.*

*What is the meaning of this conversation?*

*How can I apply this to my daily life?*

*How can I do it successfully?*

*What is the action being called for?*

*What actions will I take?*

*How can I apply this to my family?*

# CONVERSATION #1

## SELLING IS ALL ABOUT LIFE

*All of life is about selling something.*
*It could be a service, a product,*
*a concept or even a simple idea.*
*It could be motivating others*
*to move in a different direction.*
*It could even be selling you to yourself*
*for that is the most important sale you can ever make.*
*Once you make that sale, you're on your way to greater success.*

*You see, selling is about life itself.*
*It's about connecting. It's about understanding.*
*It's about interacting. It's about listening.*
*It's about sensing what people need*
*and want most, then delivering.*
*It's about belief in oneself*
*and The One up above.*
*In the end,*
*success*
*depends on ability*
*to communicate,*
*what one says, how one says it,*
*what is heard and more importantly, what is felt.*

### SELLING IS SIMPLE
### SELL WHAT YOU HAVE INSIDE FIRST

# THOUGHTS & ACTIONS

*Gain lasting results from this conversation by asking
yourself the following questions and noting your answers.*

**What is the meaning of this conversation?**

**How can I apply this to my daily life?**

**How can I do it successfully?**

**What is the action being called for?**

**What actions will I take?**

**How can I apply this to my family?**

# CONVERSATION #2

## IT'S WHAT'S INSIDE THAT COUNTS™

*It's not how tall or short you are.*

*It's not how rich or poor you are.*

*It's not how thin or curvaceous you are.*

*It's not how beautiful, handsome or plain you are.*

*It's not how white, brown, yellow or black you are.*

*It's not how famous or unknown you are.*

*It's not even how young or old you are.*

*IT'S WHAT'S INSIDE THAT COUNTS™*

*It's what you have done.*

*It's what you are capable of doing.*

*It's who you are destined to become.*

*It's your character, values, heart and soul.*

*It's integrity, trust, comfort and how much you care.*

*It's what you give of yourself to those in need.*

*It's all that makes you stand out in a crowd.*

*It's all about believing in what you have.*

## APPRECIATE
## WHAT YOU HAVE INSIDE

# THOUGHTS & ACTIONS

*Gain lasting results from this conversation by asking yourself the following questions and noting your answers.*

### What is the meaning of this conversation?

### How can I apply this to my daily life?

### How can I do it successfully?

### What is the action being called for?

### What actions will I take?

### How can I apply this to my family?

# CONVERSATION #3

## ONLY TURN THE WHEEL ENOUGH
## TO GET AROUND THE CORNER

*When attempting to persuade someone to do, change or buy something,*

*only turn the wheel enough to get around the "corner".*

*Once the car is going in the right direction,*

*leave the steering wheel alone*

*before you bump into a curb.*

*You've arrived - you're there,*

*you've succeeded,*

*you have an agreement.*

*Don't say another word.*

### JUST SIT BACK AND ENJOY THE RIDE

# THOUGHTS & ACTIONS

*Gain lasting results from this conversation by asking yourself the following questions and noting your answers.*

*What is the meaning of this conversation?*

*How can I apply this to my daily life?*

*How can I do it successfully?*

*What is the action being called for?*

*What actions will I take?*

*How can I apply this to my family?*

# CONVERSATION #4

## WISDOM IS IN A CLASS BY ITSELF
*Wisdom is the ability to act with complete confidence using knowledge,*

*experience, understanding, common sense and insight.*

*Wisdom knows when to speak, or remain silent,*

*when to listen, when to understand,*

*when to help, when to reach out,*

*or when to ignore and forgive*

*boisterous ignorance.*

*Wisdom is self-sufficient,*

*inclusive and welcoming.*
## WISDOM IS A RARE GIFT
## USE IT WISELY

# THOUGHTS & ACTIONS

*Gain lasting results from this conversation by asking yourself the following questions and noting your answers.*

### What is the meaning of this conversation?

### How can I apply this to my daily life?

### How can I do it successfully?

### What is the action being called for?

### What actions will I take?

### How can I apply this to my family?

# CONVERSATION #5

## WHAT WOULD HAPPEN IF YOU MET YOURSELF AT A PARTY?

What would your reaction be if you met yourself
for the very first time? What would you say?
More importantly, what would you feel?
Would you like the person you just met?
How confident would you feel?
When you talk to yourself,
do you think of yourself as a friend,
a lover, an antagonist, an adversary,
an enemy or are you just a reflection
of a historical voice from the past?
We talk with ourselves all day and
it's important to watch
what we say and
how we say it
to ourselves.
Once you truly
believe in yourself,
introduce you to yourself.
Get to really know each other.
Make a great new friend for life.
**"YOU WERE MEANT FOR ME"**

# THOUGHTS & ACTIONS

*Gain lasting results from this conversation by asking yourself the following questions and noting your answers.*

### What is the meaning of this conversation?

### How can I apply this to my daily life?

### How can I do it successfully?

### What is the action being called for?

### What actions will I take?

### How can I apply this to my family?

# CONVERSATION #6

## TURN ON YOUR RED LIGHT

*Sometimes you just must pretend.*

*Pretend? I know, but do it anyway.*

*Pretend you have a red light*

*hidden deep inside your chest.*

*It's waiting to be turned on at your command.*

*When you turn on your red light, you ignite a mysterious,*

*powerful ray that penetrates whomever you're standing next to.*

*When you turn on your red light, people will not be able to resist*

*what you say or how you say it.*

*When you turn on your red light, you'll project an instant surge*

*of power and confidence not present before.*

*This is the power of the red light.*

*It's the power of self-belief.*

*It's the power of self-confidence.*

*Once you truly believe it's there,*

*everything begins to change.*

*All you do is*

*pretend and turn it on.*

*Belief Soon Becomes a Reality!*

## DISCOVER WHAT CAN HAPPEN
## WHEN YOU BELIEVE

# THOUGHTS & ACTIONS

*Gain lasting results from this conversation by asking yourself the following questions and noting your answers.*

**What is the meaning of this conversation?**

**How can I apply this to my daily life?**

**How can I do it successfully?**

**What is the action being called for?**

**What actions will I take?**

**How can I apply this to my family?**

# CONVERSATION #7

## IMPRESS THEM IN THE FIRST TEN SECONDS

*How do you impress a potential client in the first ten seconds?*

*Well, you might want to do a hand stand in the middle of the office.*

*Or you might want to suddenly open with a funny song in the wrong key.*

*If that didn't work, prepare to do something that will really get their attention.*

*When you enter their office for the first time, don't say a word.*

*Slowly look around the room and assess everything you see.*

*Now look at the whole person from top to bottom.*

*Assess once again exactly what you see.*

*Next look directly into his/her eyes.*

*Assess intently what you see.*

*Now reach out*

*with a firm handshake.*

*Totally assess what you feel.*

*Then and only then should you speak.*

## MAKE THIS YOUR "HELLO" MOMENT

# THOUGHTS & ACTIONS

*Gain lasting results from this conversation by asking yourself the following questions and noting your answers.*

*What is the meaning of this conversation?*

*How can I apply this to my daily life?*

*How can I do it successfully?*

*What is the action being called for?*

*What actions will I take?*

*How can I apply this to my family?*

# CONVERSATION #8

## BUILD YOUR LIFE AROUND SEVEN PILLARS OF STRENGTH

*TRUST has but one level. It's either there or it isn't.
It never comes in degrees or shades of gray. It's never loud or soft.
It silently weaves a bond between human beings that once broken is rarely,
if ever, put back together again. It's the highest attribute of the human state.*

*COMMITMENT has its place with those who strive for excellence.
It's a promise to do more, to give more, to perform at the peak of one's ability.
It becomes a word of honor, a solemn pledge to go beyond the norm. It is the single
most important ingredient in the achievement of success.*

*RESPECT is something you give before you can receive. It controls the way we
communicate and treat each other. It is the one thing everybody wants, but not
everyone receives. It is the highest compliment one can give another.*

*KNOWLEDGE is something you acquire. It is not a gift. It is earned through study
and hard work. It's more than facts and information. It is the ability to absorb and
comprehend the changing world around us. It stems from
intelligence and a desire to seek the truth.*

*LEADERSHIP either acts or motivates action. It is the act of influencing or guiding
one in a specific direction. It originates from power.
Good leadership is the wise use of this power.*

*ENERGY is the fuel. It is the power and the stamina to do more, to excel. It is the
will to do whatever it takes to get the job done and get it done right.
It is the driving force that propels one to reach new heights.*

*COMPASSION is an emotional response one human being has for another. It is a
deep understanding of the feelings and concerns one might have. It can calm stormy
seas and quiet the winds. It can reach the inner part of the human condition.*

## CREATE THIS FOUNDATION FOR SUCCESS
## AND YOU WILL SOON KNOW GREATNESS

# THOUGHTS & ACTIONS

*Gain lasting results from this conversation by asking
yourself the following questions and noting your answers.*

**What is the meaning of this conversation?**

**How can I apply this to my daily life?**

**How can I do it successfully?**

**What is the action being called for?**

**What actions will I take?**

**How can I apply this to my family?**

## CONVERSATION #9

### THIS IS THE MOMENT

*Did you ever wonder*

*how many moments*

*The One up above*

*allotted to each of us?*

*How valuable would they be*

*if you knew exactly how many*

*you were given and more importantly,*

*how many were left to enjoy in your life?*

*If you knew, everything*

*in your life would change.*


*Don't leave a moment go by!*

*Be there in the moment.*

*Expand the moment.*

*Make the moment*

*what you want it to be.*

*Explore the moment.*

*Make the moment memorable.*

*Make the moment unforgettable.*

*This moment will never happen again.*

### DON'T FORGET THIS MOMENT
### SOMETHING TO THINK ABOUT

# THOUGHTS & ACTIONS

*Gain lasting results from this conversation by asking
yourself the following questions and noting your answers.*


*What is the meaning of this conversation?*


*How can I apply this to my daily life?*


*How can I do it successfully?*


*What is the action being called for?*


*What actions will I take?*


*How can I apply this to my family?*

## CONVERSATION #10

### SELF-CONFIDENCE IS LIKE A VERY DRY MARTINI

*It can rapidly make you feel very good inside.*

*It can bring out your most humorous side.*

*It can magnify strong feelings of power.*

*It can at times be a bit intoxicating.*

*It can also provide the courage*

*to attempt the impossible,*

*then finding it possible.*

*When that happens,*

*It becomes*

*the secret*

*for success.*

**SIP SLOWLY**

# THOUGHTS & ACTIONS

*Gain lasting results from this conversation by asking yourself the following questions and noting your answers.*

**What is the meaning of this conversation?**

**How can I apply this to my daily life?**

**How can I do it successfully?**

**What is the action being called for?**

**What actions will I take?**

**How can I apply this to my family?**

# CONVERSATION #11

## OPEN UP YOUR LIFE

Listen to the crashing waves.

Listen to the song they sing.

Open all the doors.

Open all the windows.

Let the Light shine in and enlighten you.

Let soft, ocean breezes of inspiration surround and empower you.

Take a deep breath, sit back

and just listen!
## SET YOURSELF FREE

# THOUGHTS & ACTIONS

*Gain lasting results from this conversation by asking
yourself the following questions and noting your answers.*

*What is the meaning of this conversation?*

*How can I apply this to my daily life?*

*How can I do it successfully?*

*What is the action being called for?*

*What actions will I take?*

*How can I apply this to my family?*

# CONVERSATION #12

## SUCCESS IN LIFE IS LIKE OWNING A CAR

You have a vehicle that takes you

anywhere you want to go day or night.

But the car doesn't move until you decide you want it to move.

All you need to do is decide when, where and how fast you want to go.

Nothing happens until you turn on the engine and press the accelerator.

Otherwise, you'll just sit there until you decide to make it happen.

Sit there long enough and notice other cars are passing you by.

"Where are they going, you ask?"

It seems they're moving

faster and faster

as they pass you by.

Success in life is like owning a car.

It's there for you to take wherever you want to go.

All you must do is decide where you want to go and then act.

### NOTHING HAPPENS UNTIL YOU ACT!

If you notice cars are passing you by, maybe now is a good time to act.

It's time to finally realize, your car will take you anywhere you want to go.

All you have to do is start your engine, press on the accelerator and move.

By the way, now would be a good time to act before traffic gets too heavy.

## LADIES AND GENTLEMEN, START UP YOUR ENGINES
## THE RACE IS ABOUT TO BEGIN

# THOUGHTS & ACTIONS

*Gain lasting results from this conversation by asking yourself the following questions and noting your answers.*

*What is the meaning of this conversation?*

*How can I apply this to my daily life?*

*How can I do it successfully?*

*What is the action being called for?*

*What actions will I take?*

*How can I apply this to my family?*

# CONVERSATION #13

## CREATIVE MARKETING IS LIKE COMPOSING A SYMPHONY

Like composing a symphony, great marketing follows a creative formula.

What you see, hear and feel in a symphony is precisely composed

and orchestrated to create a compelling emotional response.

Each player has a part spelled out note for note in total

harmony of sounds and colors with the rest.

It starts with a main theme or melody,

followed by variations to that theme.

It's designed to build intense

desires, emotions, intrigue,

understanding and depth.

When the story has been unfolded,

the entire orchestra comes together

in a celebration with a climax that makes

the whole experience totally unforgettable.

It's expertly brought to life at the direction

of a conductor in total control of the tempo,

emotions, dynamics and responses to what

is heard and especially to what is felt.

### PENETRATE WITH THE RIGHT THEME
### AND THE MELODY WILL LINGER FOREVER

# THOUGHTS & ACTIONS

*Gain lasting results from this conversation by asking yourself the following questions and noting your answers.*

*What is the meaning of this conversation?*

*How can I apply this to my daily life?*

*How can I do it successfully?*

*What is the action being called for?*

*What actions will I take?*

*How can I apply this to my family?*

# CONVERSATION #14

## GIVE A "PEACE" OF CHOCOLATE
*Make life simple.*

*Discover what's important.*

*Do whatever you need to do*

*to bring happiness to the one*

*you love and yourself.*

*Declare to your other, "My purpose in this life is to make you happy."*

*Now do whatever it takes that will give proof to what you just said.*

*Make it your dedication and your commitment. Make it your goal.*

*Now imagine you both saying and doing this every single day.*

*By the way, you might want to give to each other*

*a piece of chocolate as a gift when you say it.*

*Try it together and feel what happens.*

*Keep doing it until there is*

*total belief in the words.*

*Don't be surprised*

*by the rewards*

*you receive.*

*The result is pure happiness, peace and tranquillity.*

*When you have these, you have life on a much different level.*

### AFTER ALL, WHAT ELSE IS THERE
### TRY IT! YOU'LL LIKE IT!

# THOUGHTS & ACTIONS

*Gain lasting results from this conversation by asking yourself the following questions and noting your answers.*

### What is the meaning of this conversation?

### How can I apply this to my daily life?

### How can I do it successfully?

### What is the action being called for?

### What actions will I take?

### How can I apply this to my family?

# CONVERSATION #15

## THE BRIDGE OF TRUST

Establish Trust and They Will Visit.

Build A Bridge of Trust and They Will Freely Flow Back and Forth.

Add Comfort and They Will Stay.

TRUST & COMFORT

The two most powerful words

in life, in sales and in marketing.

## PREPARE FOR A CROWD
## GET OUT THE GOOD DISHES

# THOUGHTS & ACTIONS

*Gain lasting results from this conversation by asking yourself the following questions and noting your answers.*

### What is the meaning of this conversation?

### How can I apply this to my daily life?

### How can I do it successfully?

### What is the action being called for?

### What actions will I take?

### How can I apply this to my family?

# CONVERSATION #16

## IT HAPPENS EVERYTIME

*Success never happens by accident.*

*It happens because it was planned.*

*It happens because a plan was executed.*

*It happens because you made it happen.*

*It happens because you willed it to happen.*

*It happens because you allowed it to happen.*

*It happens because you finally felt*

*you deserved to have it happen.*

*Can you make it happen?*

*"Yes, I can."*

*Say it again.*

*"Yes, I can."*

## NOW WATCH WHAT HAPPENS

# THOUGHTS & ACTIONS

*Gain lasting results from this conversation by asking yourself the following questions and noting your answers.*

## What is the meaning of this conversation?

## How can I apply this to my daily life?

## How can I do it successfully?

## What is the action being called for?

## What actions will I take?

## How can I apply this to my family?

# CONVERSATION #17

## PRETEND YOU ARE THE HONORED GUEST
### YESTERDAY
*Walk into a party of people with great apprehension.*
*Move very cautiously, react in a passive way.*
*Walk and greet people in a reluctant way.*
*Continually project a lack of confidence.*
*Receive a cold reception based upon*
*initial apprehension and behavior.*
*How did you greet people?*
*How did they react?*
*How did it feel?*

### TODAY
*Enter the same party and*
*pretend you are now the honored guest.*
*Pretend everyone is waiting for you to arrive.*
*Pretend everyone wants to talk with you, be with you.*
*Watch their response as you make numerous personal contacts,*
*greeting each of them with self-confidence, bestowing small talk,*
*moving rapidly from person to person, each waiting just for you.*
*How did that feel?*
*Did you do anything*
*different from before?*
*How did they respond?*

## CONFIDENCE IS A STATE OF MIND
## PRETEND UNTIL IT BECOMES YOUR REALITY

# THOUGHTS & ACTIONS

*Gain lasting results from this conversation by asking yourself the following questions and noting your answers.*

*What is the meaning of this conversation?*

*How can I apply this to my daily life?*

*How can I do it successfully?*

*What is the action being called for?*

*What actions will I take?*

*How can I apply this to my family?*

# CONVERSATION #18

## SPARK A LIVE CONNECTION

*And see what life is all about.*

*Connect with the ocean*

*as far as you can see.*

*Connect with life so*

*you can be free.*

*Connect with people*

*and help them to be.*

*Connect with The One up*

*above so that you can believe.*

*Connect with your eyes so that you*

*can then see what is hidden deep inside.*

*Great relationships*

*are achieved by connecting with the eyes.*

*Positive interactions start when your eyes first meet.*

*Follow the eyes wherever they go. Look in them deeply,*

*approvingly and emotionally. Finally, look in them intellectually.*

*Do not leave them until you feel you have made a penetrating connection.*

### "ON A CLEAR DAY YOU CAN SEE FOREVER"
### TRY IT AND SEE

# THOUGHTS & ACTIONS

*Gain lasting results from this conversation by asking yourself the following questions and noting your answers.*

### What is the meaning of this conversation?

### How can I apply this to my daily life?

### How can I do it successfully?

### What is the action being called for?

### What actions will I take?

### How can I apply this to my family?

# CONVERSATION #19

## WIN THE KEYS TO THE CASTLE

*When you have the key to the castle,*

*you'll discover what's inside.*

*You'll find it's all there*

*for you to have*

*and share.*

*It's self-belief.*

*It's self-knowledge.*

*It's self-appreciation.*

*It's total self-confidence.*

*It's understanding who you are.*

*It's belief and faith in The One up above.*

*In the end, you have the key that unlocks success.*

## DISCOVER IT ALL BEFORE IT'S TOO LATE

# THOUGHTS & ACTIONS

*Gain lasting results from this conversation by asking yourself the following questions and noting your answers.*

**What is the meaning of this conversation?**

**How can I apply this to my daily life?**

**How can I do it successfully?**

**What is the action being called for?**

**What actions will I take?**

**How can I apply this to my family?**

# CONVERSATION #20

## "WHAT IS THIS THING CALLED LOVE"

*Don't sell things.*

*Nobody buys things.*

*Nobody really buys benefits of things.*

*They buy the feelings benefits of things bring.*

*Tell the story about the feelings of things.*

*Make it real.*

*Make it emotional.*

*Make it believable.*

*Define the feelings*

*benefits deliver.*

*Nothing else is important.*

*Nothing else really matters.*

*Open what feelings bring and*

*you will soon open the door to success.*

## TOUCH THE FEELINGS THINGS BRING

# THOUGHTS & ACTIONS

*Gain lasting results from this conversation by asking yourself the following questions and noting your answers.*

## What is the meaning of this conversation?

## How can I apply this to my daily life?

## How can I do it successfully?

## What is the action being called for?

## What actions will I take?

## How can I apply this to my family?

# CONVERSATION #21

## MAKE ROOM FOR A FULL LIFE

*Life is like a beautiful house*
*with many different rooms for you to enter,*
*live and grow before moving on to yet another.*
*The past is locked in a room you lived in long ago.*
*When you feel the need to go back to "memory lane",*
*review, adjust past perceptions, forgive yourself, then lock the door.*
*Absolutely nothing can be done about the past for it is now the past.*
*You are now living in a brand new, larger and much brighter room.*
*Think about exploring, engaging and enjoying that which is in*
*your new room before preparing to move on.*
*Happiness is just a few small steps away.*

*Life is about growth!*
*Life is about moving ahead!*
*Life is about how many times we got back up and succeeded.*
*Getting back up and moving forward is the key.*
*It's a time to forgive, forget and move up.*
*It's time to make room for a full life.*

## DON'T WASTE A MINUTE ON THE PAST
## SPEND A LIFETIME ON YOUR FUTURE

# THOUGHTS & ACTIONS

*Gain lasting results from this conversation by asking
yourself the following questions and noting your answers.*

### What is the meaning of this conversation?

### How can I apply this to my daily life?

### How can I do it successfully?

### What is the action being called for?

### What actions will I take?

### How can I apply this to my family?

# CONVERSATION #22

## WORDS ARE JUST WORDS
*No matter how many words you hear,*

*words don't always say what they mean.*

*Words by themselves can be very misleading.*

*Instead...*

*"Listen" for the pain.*

*"Listen" for the needs.*

*"Listen" for the concerns.*

*"Listen" for the desires.*

*"Listen" for the feelings.*

*Most important,*

*"Listen" for the soul hidden deep inside.*
## DON'T STOP UNTIL YOU "HEAR"
## WHAT'S INSIDE

# THOUGHTS & ACTIONS

*Gain lasting results from this conversation by asking yourself the following questions and noting your answers.*

**What is the meaning of this conversation?**

**How can I apply this to my daily life?**

**How can I do it successfully?**

**What is the action being called for?**

**What actions will I take?**

**How can I apply this to my family?**

# CONVERSATION #23

## RUB THE GOLDEN LAMP

*What would happen if you had a Genie*
*available to you and all you had to do was*
*rub the golden lamp and state your wishes?*
*Your Genie would magically appear and say,*
*"Yes master, what do you desire today?"*

*That's what your subconscious mind does. It's your personal Genie.*
*It just sits there, waiting for orders from you. Then it delivers.*
*Sometimes it delivers more than what was asked, so be careful!*
*Whatever the conscious mind continually thinks about*
*and believes to be true,*
*the subconscious mind accepts,*
*acts and then delivers.*
*It delivers just like the Genie says.*

## RUB IT LIKE YOU MEAN IT
## AND THEN WATCH WHAT HAPPENS

# THOUGHTS & ACTIONS

*Gain lasting results from this conversation by asking yourself the following questions and noting your answers.*

*What is the meaning of this conversation?*

*How can I apply this to my daily life?*

*How can I do it successfully?*

*What is the action being called for?*

*What actions will I take?*

*How can I apply this to my family?*

# CONVERSATION #24

## EVERYONE WAS TWENTYSOMETHING AT ONE TIME
*Older folks walk along the beach at sunset*

*strolling slowly so that they can fully enjoy*

*the beauty and the ambiance before them.*

*Look deeply into those elderly standing before you.*

*Don't forget...they were all twentysomethings at one time.*

*They were the brightest lights.*

*The crazy dancing music sights.*

*The captured love from up above.*

*The happy-go-lucky beautiful greats.*

*The ones with attitude, freedom and*

*conviction that gave them what they desired.*

*See them as they once were, it's who they really are down deep inside.*

## IT IS NOT THAT FAR FROM WHERE YOU ARE

# THOUGHTS & ACTIONS

*Gain lasting results from this conversation by asking yourself the following questions and noting your answers.*

*What is the meaning of this conversation?*

*How can I apply this to my daily life?*

*How can I do it successfully?*

*What is the action being called for?*

*What actions will I take?*

*How can I apply this to my family?*

# CONVERSATION #25

## DON'T GET CAUGHT IN THE RAIN

How many times have you tried to help someone and got caught in the rain?

Try this!

"Because I love you, I want to suggest something that might help you with....."

When the forecast is for a stormy conversation,

always open your umbrella just before starting.

Your umbrella is a statement of truth and love

that justifies and softens what is to follow.

It re-establishes and re-connects a positive

emotional attachment with the person by

showing respect, love, confidence,

value or endearment before

you evaluate, correct, teach

or even suggest change.

Open your umbrella

when needing cover

from the rain.

Try it now.

It works.

It protects!

It's smart!

## "START SINGING IN THE RAIN"

# THOUGHTS & ACTIONS

*Gain lasting results from this conversation by asking yourself the following questions and noting your answers.*

*What is the meaning of this conversation?*

*How can I apply this to my daily life?*

*How can I do it successfully?*

*What is the action being called for?*

*What actions will I take?*

*How can I apply this to my family?*

# CONVERSATION #26

## SLAY THE UGLY MONSTERS

*Every problem is not a problem.*

*Every failure is not a failure.*

*Every refusal is not a refusal,*

*not when you put them in proper perspective.*

*Take a piece of paper and place a small dot in its center.*

*Hold the paper up close until the dot looks larger than it really is.*

*Now lower the paper and place it on the floor in the center of a large room.*

*Slowly walk away from the dot in the center to the far side of the room.*

*Notice how small it begins to appear relative to everything else in the room.*

*NOW PRETEND THE DOT IS YOUR LATEST "PROBLEM".*

*Walk away from the problem until you are on the larger side of your life.*

*How big is the "problem" relative to everything you have going in your life?*

*If the dot was your problem, would that small dot now change your life?*

*Look upon your "problems" with the same perspective.*

*Would any of them make a difference in your life?*

*Try it! Will you try it? Say yes.*

*Say it again and again until you begin*

*to minimize all the "problems" in your life*

*with a new level of self-confidence,*

*perspective and success.*

*What happens to you is not as important*

*as how you respond to what happens to you.*

## SLAY THE UGLY MONSTERS
## BE IN CONTROL

# THOUGHTS & ACTIONS

*Gain lasting results from this conversation by asking
yourself the following questions and noting your answers.*

### What is the meaning of this conversation?

### How can I apply this to my daily life?

### How can I do it successfully?

### What is the action being called for?

### What actions will I take?

### How can I apply this to my family?

# CONVERSATION #27

## ACT NOW OR FOREVER HOLD YOUR PAST

*When there is a need to move forward,*

*don't just say what you want to do!*

*Actions speak louder than words!*

*Just do what you need to do!*

*They define why you are here*

*and what you hold dear.*

*Actions define who you are.*

*They lay the foundation for success.*

*It's what you do – not what you say.*

*It's the actions you take, not what you preach.*

*Actions will make all the difference in your world*

*for words define what you did, not what you will do.*

*Select one action that will immediately improve your life.*

### CREATE AN UNFORGETTABLE BLOCKBUSTER
### LIGHTS - CAMERA – ACTION

# THOUGHTS & ACTIONS

*Gain lasting results from this conversation by asking
yourself the following questions and noting your answers.*

**What is the meaning of this conversation?**

**How can I apply this to my daily life?**

**How can I do it successfully?**

**What is the action being called for?**

**What actions will I take?**

**How can I apply this to my family?**

## CONVERSATION #28

### IGNITE WHAT YOU WANT AND NEED IN LIFE
*Life is simple.*

*All you must do is*

*ignite what you want in life.*

*Give it life – substance – size –*

*importance – and permanence.*

*Then begin to give it all away.*

*Become an igniter!*

*If you want trust, you must first ignite trust.*

*If you want respect, you must first ignite respect.*

*If you want love, you must first ignite the flame of love.*

### WHATEVER YOU IGNITE IN YOUR LIFE BECOMES AN IMPORTANT PART OF YOU FOR THE REST OF YOUR LIFE

# THOUGHTS & ACTIONS

*Gain lasting results from this conversation by asking yourself the following questions and noting your answers.*

**What is the meaning of this conversation?**

**How can I apply this to my daily life?**

**How can I do it successfully?**

**What is the action being called for?**

**What actions will I take?**

**How can I apply this to my family?**

## CONVERSATION #29

*LET IT BE SAID*
*YOU CAN NOW BE HAPPY ALL THE TIME*
*If you really want to be happy,*

*schedule a specific hour each day when you plan to be unusually happy.*

*First smile, then tell yourself, "I am about to become extremely happy."*

*Don't let anything or anyone prevent you from reaching that goal.*

*Once you achieve it, expand that to an hour and a half.*

*Once you achieve that, expand it to two hours*

*then to three hours. Once you achieve that,*

*expand it even more.*

*Can you do that?*

*Say it! "I can do that."*

*Now smile and say it*

*one more time.*

*"I can do that."*
**IMAGINE WHERE THIS COULD TAKE YOU**

# THOUGHTS & ACTIONS

*Gain lasting results from this conversation by asking yourself the following questions and noting your answers.*


*What is the meaning of this conversation?*


*How can I apply this to my daily life?*


*How can I do it successfully?*


*What is the action being called for?*


*What actions will I take?*


*How can I apply this to my family?*

# CONVERSATION #30

## TALK YOURSELF INTO IT
*If I told you that your success
depends on what you say to yourself
every minute, every hour and every day of your life
you would change every aspect of your internal conversation.
Whatever you feed into your brain will sooner or later be reflected
as what you do and how well you do it. So, become a positive influence
on yourself. Become your own motivator, your own best friend saluting
your successes, your accomplishments and all that you achieve.*

*Make "Yes I can!" part of your personality.
For starters, take control now of your desire for success.
It all starts with the repetition of what you say to yourself.*

*Eliminate negatives about
your person, your personality,
your body, your mind, your values, your past,
your intelligence or even your ability to succeed.
Talk to yourself with positive reinforcement of your abilities.
Use short positive statements that begin with: I am..., I will..., I can....,
I did..., I know..., I care..., I'm going to..., I believe..., I expect..., I promise...,
I'm strong..., I'm special. Complete each with a sentence that will establish
a winning feeling with the person inside – and that is you. Now repeat as often
as you can until they are etched into your sub-conscious mind. Allow them to
become part of who you are and dictate what you will do and how you will do
it. Become a reflection of what you say to yourself every day.
Become your own best friend.*
### YOU CAN TALK YOURSELF INTO ANYTHING
### ONCE YOU TRULY BELIEVE YOU CAN
### TRY IT AND SEE

# THOUGHTS & ACTIONS

*Gain lasting results from this conversation by asking yourself the following questions and noting your answers.*

*What is the meaning of this conversation?*

*How can I apply this to my daily life?*

*How can I do it successfully?*

*What is the action being called for?*

*What actions will I take?*

*How can I apply this to my family?*

# CONVERSATION #31

*FALL IN LOVE*
*ONE MORE TIME*
*Learn how to love!*

*Learn how to love yourself.*

*Become a distributor of love.*

*Become a pure reflection of love.*

*Project love to anyone and everyone.*

*Enable feelings to fill your consciousness.*

*Allow it always to show in the way you talk,*

*the way you walk and*

*the way you move.*

*Permit it to fill your being until the totality of you begins*

*to communicate the most important attribute in the Universe.*
*TRUE LOVE IS A GIFT*
*GIVEN FROM DEEP INSIDE*
*WRAP CAREFULLY*

# THOUGHTS & ACTIONS

*Gain lasting results from this conversation by asking yourself the following questions and noting your answers.*

*What is the meaning of this conversation?*

*How can I apply this to my daily life?*

*How can I do it successfully?*

*What is the action being called for?*

*What actions will I take?*

*How can I apply this to my family?*

# CONVERSATION #32

## *YOUR BODY SPEAKS LOUDER THAN WORDS*
*There was not even a sound*

*that would have given you a clue*

*but the message was still there.*

*From your body,*

*it relentlessly projected,*

*what you wished would not be revealed.*

*Make sure you are fully aware*

*when your mind is in despair.*

*You might be sending the wrong message*

*to those close by.*

## *WATCH OUT*
## *FOR WHAT YOU DIDN'T SAY IS "HEARD"*
## *AND "UNDERSTOOD"*

# THOUGHTS & ACTIONS

*Gain lasting results from this conversation by asking yourself the following questions and noting your answers.*

*What is the meaning of this conversation?*

*How can I apply this to my daily life?*

*How can I do it successfully?*

*What is the action being called for?*

*What actions will I take?*

*How can I apply this to my family?*

## CONVERSATION #33

### DON'T EVER SAY NO

Don't say "no". "No" locks down all the gates to success. "No" is easy.
It is safe, passive and leads to doing nothing. "Yes" is courageous.
It calls for leadership, exploration, action,
hard work with the possibility of
great success and sometimes,
even failure.
Instead, say maybe, possibly, could be, might be,
great idea, let's think about it, when can we start,
let's find a way to do it.
Make sure the welcoming gates
of opportunity remain open.
Can you do that? Say Yes.
Say it one more time. Yes!
### YOU'LL BE SURPRISED
### WHAT A YES CAN DO FOR YOU

# THOUGHTS & ACTIONS

*Gain lasting results from this conversation by asking yourself the following questions and noting your answers.*

**What is the meaning of this conversation?**

**How can I apply this to my daily life?**

**How can I do it successfully?**

**What is the action being called for?**

**What actions will I take?**

**How can I apply this to my family?**

## CONVERSATION #34

### HAPPINESS IS NO LONGER A RARE COMMODITY
*Sometimes you just have to give something away to be happy.*

*Try this next time you feel the need for greater happiness.*

*Pick out one person that you are close to and*

*think about what would make*

*him or her most happy - today.*

*Once you discover what it is,*

*create a plan on how you will*

*bestow this bit of happiness.*

*Wait until the time is right and*

*then deliver without hesitation.*

*Watch with satisfaction the feelings*

*of happiness you just gave away.*

*How did it make the person feel?*

*Now just wait for their response.*

*How happy did this make you feel?*

*Maybe, just maybe, you found the secret.*

*If you want to be happier,*

*try this on another person tomorrow.*

*If your level of happiness is now expanding,*

*try it on another – and another – and another.*

*Before you get too giddy, rest a day and continue as needed.*

*Can you do that? Say it now. "I can do that."*

*Say it one more time but with a smile. "I can do that."*

### SPREAD HAPPINESS AROUND YOU
### AND IT WILL ASTOUND YOU

# THOUGHTS & ACTIONS

*Gain lasting results from this conversation by asking yourself the following questions and noting your answers.*

### What is the meaning of this conversation?

### How can I apply this to my daily life?

### How can I do it successfully?

### What is the action being called for?

### What actions will I take?

### How can I apply this to my family?

# CONVERSATION #35

## PLANT A GARDEN OF SUCCESS

*Success in life is much like planting a garden.*

*You have a fertile garden in the back of your mind.*

*It's ready, willing and waiting to grow whatever you plant.*

*Just plant the right seeds for what you desire and watch them grow.*

*Plant some beliefs and lots of values. Plant your vision and a few goals.*

*Plant some compassion, inspiration and trust.*

*Give them tender, loving care each day.*

*Make sure you protect them from weeds of despair,*

*but remember, nothing will happen until you plant the seeds.*

*Make use of the fertile garden you possess in the back of your mind.*

### PLANT SMALL SEEDS OF SUCCESS NOW
### HARVEST TIME WILL SOON BE HERE

# THOUGHTS & ACTIONS

*Gain lasting results from this conversation by asking yourself the following questions and noting your answers.*

*What is the meaning of this conversation?*

*How can I apply this to my daily life?*

*How can I do it successfully?*

*What is the action being called for?*

*What actions will I take?*

*How can I apply this to my family?*

## CONVERSATION #36

*WHY OH WHY DO YOU WORRY ALL THE TIME?*
*When you are bothered with too many worries,*

*list and prioritize what you're worried about without delay.*

*Now, schedule a special time to only worry about them*

*each Wednesday from 9:00 to 10:00 AM.*

*Notice, by the time Wednesday comes around,*

*many of your worries will have taken care of themselves.*

*So why worry?*

*SET A TIME TO WORRY*
*BEFORE IT'S TOO LATE*

# THOUGHTS & ACTIONS

*Gain lasting results from this conversation by asking yourself the following questions and noting your answers.*

*What is the meaning of this conversation?*

*How can I apply this to my daily life?*

*How can I do it successfully?*

*What is the action being called for?*

*What actions will I take?*

*How can I apply this to my family?*

# CONVERSATION #37

## BIG DOGS DON'T BARK

*Big dogs don't bark.*
*Why? They don't have to.*
*Like those who are strong and powerful,*
*they never say they are with words.*
*Why? They don't have to.*
*They show it with actions.*

*Have you also noticed?*
*Small dogs bark incessantly.*
*Why? They know they must.*
*Like those who are weak and afraid,*
*they're constantly trying to tell*
*how strong and powerful they are.*
*Why? They know they need to.*

## BARK SOFTLY
## ACT LOUDLY

# THOUGHTS & ACTIONS

*Gain lasting results from this conversation by asking yourself the following questions and noting your answers.*

*What is the meaning of this conversation?*

*How can I apply this to my daily life?*

*How can I do it successfully?*

*What is the action being called for?*

*What actions will I take?*

*How can I apply this to my family?*

# CONVERSATION #38

## IT'S ALL ABOUT KNOWING
*Success!*

*It's about knowing how.*

*Knowing where you've been.*

*Knowing where you want to go.*

*Knowing precisely where you are now.*

*Knowing what you need to do to get there.*

*Knowing how and when you'll finally arrive.*

### KNOWING IS THE POWER TO BE
### TO SEE AND TO BE FREE
### JUST KNOW IT

# THOUGHTS & ACTIONS

*Gain lasting results from this conversation by asking yourself the following questions and noting your answers.*

*What is the meaning of this conversation?*

*How can I apply this to my daily life?*

*How can I do it successfully?*

*What is the action being called for?*

*What actions will I take?*

*How can I apply this to my family?*

## CONVERSATION #39

### WAIT UNTIL THE WEATHER CHANGES
*If you're looking for change,*

*don't change where you live,*

*don't change where you work and*

*don't change with whom you're with.*

*In fact, don't even make a move until you*

*first change the weather hovering above you.*

*Otherwise, absolutely nothing will change.*

*"Your" weather, be it good or bad,*

*will stay with you*

**wherever you go.**

**EVERYTHING GETS BETTER
WHEN THE SUN IS SHINING ABOVE YOU**

# THOUGHTS & ACTIONS

*Gain lasting results from this conversation by asking yourself the following questions and noting your answers.*

### What is the meaning of this conversation?

### How can I apply this to my daily life?

### How can I do it successfully?

### What is the action being called for?

### What actions will I take?

### How can I apply this to my family?

# CONVERSATION #40

## EMBRACE REAL SUCCESS FOR ONCE

*Embrace these ten attributes and you will create more success in your life.*

*Trust, Comfort, Self-Knowledge, Self-Confidence, Self-Control, Empathy,*

*Understanding, Perseverance, Enthusiasm and Discipline.*

*Expand any one of these by any degree and you will*

*begin to increase your ability to create success.*

*Expand all of them at the same time and*

*you will be on your way*

*for some real excitement.*

## GET READY TO RUMBLE

# THOUGHTS & ACTIONS

*Gain lasting results from this conversation by asking yourself the following questions and noting your answers.*

### What is the meaning of this conversation?

### How can I apply this to my daily life?

### How can I do it successfully?

### What is the action being called for?

### What actions will I take?

### How can I apply this to my family?

# CONVERSATION #41

## FLY IN THE MAGIC BALLOON
*When a larger picture is needed,*
*when the sea sounds like rolling thunder,*
*when you need to rise above today's crazy conflicts,*
*when you need to observe, and put it all in proper perspective,*
*when you need to get above noises of strident, passionate opinions,*
*when you need to fully contemplate what is real, viable and necessary,*
*when you need to comprehend how to create empathy and understanding,*
*FLY IN THE MAGIC BALLOON.*
*Rise above the floor of life to see where you've been and where you need to go.*
*Rising higher you'll see the morning sun light up continents across the horizon.*
*Rise even higher and you will observe ancient tribal civilizations still at war.*
*Rise much higher and you will embrace a new level of peace and tranquility.*
*When you go higher, experience a rare sense of happiness and appreciation.*
*Go higher and you will now sense a new kind of wisdom that we all seek.*
*Rise above and you'll see a beautiful blue earth happily spinning at peace.*
*Out here, loud noises of conflict are suddenly silent and totally irrelevant.*
*Just A Little Bit Higher Is Paradise.*

## TRUE WISDOM ORIGINATES
## FROM AN ELEVATED
## STATE OF MIND
## RISE ABOVE IT ALL

# THOUGHTS & ACTIONS

*Gain lasting results from this conversation by asking yourself the following questions and noting your answers.*

*What is the meaning of this conversation?*

*How can I apply this to my daily life?*

*How can I do it successfully?*

*What is the action being called for?*

*What actions will I take?*

*How can I apply this to my family?*

# CONVERSATION #42

## DON'T ASK UNLESS YOU MEAN IT

*Did you ever wonder why you are here on earth?*

*Did you ever wonder if you had a real purpose in this life?*

*Ever wonder if there was something you were supposed to do in this life?*

*Did you ever wonder if there was a higher authority that placed you here?*

*Did you ever wonder if there even was a higher authority?*

*Well, wonder no longer, there is and once you know,*

*once you realize and accept, it will change your life.*

*Once you fully understand why you are here,*

*you will have a new purpose, a new strength,*

*a new level of confidence and your journey*

*will become an unforgettable adventure.*

## WONDER NO LONGER
## JUST ASK AND YOU SHALL RECEIVE

# THOUGHTS & ACTIONS

*Gain lasting results from this conversation by asking yourself the following questions and noting your answers.*

### What is the meaning of this conversation?

### How can I apply this to my daily life?

### How can I do it successfully?

### What is the action being called for?

### What actions will I take?

### How can I apply this to my family?

# CONVERSATION #43

## HARMONY BRINGS IT ALL TOGETHER
As you walk along the beach,
You can sense the real power
of waves rushing upon the shore of life.
You can feel the force of those who came before
with those of us who reach for something more.
All you can do is fit into the music of the sea
and seek ways to create greater harmony.
Being in harmony with life is the secret.

Harmony is not only the way music is arranged for our enjoyment,
it is the magic of how people come together to enhance and
expand what is seen, what is embraced and what is achieved.
Harmony enhances and expands what is heard and felt.
HARMONY BRINGS IT ALL TOGETHER
If you want to create the feeling of harmony with others
start by watching how they walk, how they talk,
how they sit and how they stand.
Watch what they do with their arms, their feet,
then watch how they hold their hands.
Model the rhythmic beat of their life.
Move how they move, stand how they stand,
do what they do with their arms and legs
and their feet, then watch what happens.
If you want to "harmonize" with people,
be in total harmony with who they are
and with who they desire to become.
You will then see in them an awareness,
a sudden "identity of self" taking place.
Do this until you feel you have created a "human connection".
This is the beginning of the closer relationship you desire.
## HARMONY IS A WAY ALL OF US CAN SING TOGETHER

# THOUGHTS & ACTIONS

*Gain lasting results from this conversation by asking yourself the following questions and noting your answers.*

### What is the meaning of this conversation?

### How can I apply this to my daily life?

### How can I do it successfully?

### What is the action being called for?

### What actions will I take?

### How can I apply this to my family?

## CONVERSATION #44

### WAVES RUSH UPON THE SHORES OF LIFE
Wave after wave rush upon the shores of life creating new beginnings.

Each generation is like a wave replacing those that came before

depositing rare gems upon the sand filled beach

while erasing footprints of the past

as they recede back into the sea,

enabling new generations

to sustain life's treasures

for yet another day.

### WHAT WAS, IS NOW
### WHAT IS NOW, WILL ALWAYS BE

# THOUGHTS & ACTIONS

*Gain lasting results from this conversation by asking yourself the following questions and noting your answers.*

*What is the meaning of this conversation?*

*How can I apply this to my daily life?*

*How can I do it successfully?*

*What is the action being called for?*

*What actions will I take?*

*How can I apply this to my family?*

# CONVERSATION #45

*NEVER SAY NEVER*
*There is one thing*
*you never want to say,*
*and that is,*
*"NEVER".*
*Never is absolute.*
*It's black or white,*
*no shades of grey.*
*It stops everything.*
*It closes all the doors*
*and all the opportunities*
*that just might come your way.*
*Life is fluid! Dynamic! It's wide open.*
*It changes every day. It accommodates*
*the present so that it fits into the future.*

*When you feel like saying never,*
*open all the windows, and all the doors.*
*Allow winds of inspiration and opportunity*
*to flow over your mind and body*
*until "never" goes away.*
*NEVER SAY NEVER*
*YOU MIGHT NOT BE ABLE*
*TO UNLOCK A DOOR*
*TO THE FUTURE*

# THOUGHTS & ACTIONS

*Gain lasting results from this conversation by asking yourself the following questions and noting your answers.*

### What is the meaning of this conversation?

### How can I apply this to my daily life?

### How can I do it successfully?

### What is the action being called for?

### What actions will I take?

### How can I apply this to my family?

# CONVERSATION #46

## "THAT AND A DIME WILL BUY
## YOU A CUP OF COFFEE"

### WHAT IS THIS?

An unforgettable response to one's highest achievements.

### WHY?

The greater your success, the more understated your response should be.

### WHY NOT?

Those who are consistently successful seldom brag about their victories.

They downplay their success as if it were an everyday occurrence.

Those with strong self-confidence always seem to attain great success

but never brag about their achievements. They don't have to.

Their actions always speak louder than words could ever tell.

When you minimize the importance of your achievements,

you increase the perception of what you achieved.

## REAL POWER IS ALWAYS UNDERSTATED
## YET INSTANTLY UNDERSTOOD

# THOUGHTS & ACTIONS

*Gain lasting results from this conversation by asking
yourself the following questions and noting your answers.*

**What is the meaning of this conversation?**

**How can I apply this to my daily life?**

**How can I do it successfully?**

**What is the action being called for?**

**What actions will I take?**

**How can I apply this to my family?**

# CONVERSATION #47

### "WHAT'S IT ALL ABOUT, ALFIE?"

*It's not about the peace of mind you desire,*
*it's about the peace of mind you give.*

*It's not about the success you have,*
*it's about the success you motivate.*

*It's not about the rules you set,*
*it's about the confidence you build.*

*It's not about the smiles you make,*
*it's about the smiles you stimulate.*

*It's not about the respect you seek,*
*it's about the respect you give.*

*It's not about the stories you tell,*
*it's about the stories you live.*

*It's not about the words you speak,*
*it's about the actions you take.*

*It's not about the trust you desire,*
*it's about the trust you show.*

*It's not about the love you seek,*
*it's about the love you create.*

*It's not about the life you live,*
*it's about the life you give.*

### WHAT'S IT ALL ABOUT
### "IT'S JUST FOR THE MOMENT WE LIVE"

# THOUGHTS & ACTIONS

*Gain lasting results from this conversation by asking yourself the following questions and noting your answers.*

**What is the meaning of this conversation?**

**How can I apply this to my daily life?**

**How can I do it successfully?**

**What is the action being called for?**

**What actions will I take?**

**How can I apply this to my family?**

# CONVERSATION #48

## HOW BAD DO YOU REALLY WANT IT?

*When you want something bad enough, there is only one rule.*

*"Whatever you want in life, visualize it,*

*embrace it, focus on its arrival and*

*assume it's already happening."*

*Now engage those actions*

*that will make it a reality.*

**IF YOU WANT IT**
**BAD ENOUGH**
**JUST DO IT**

# THOUGHTS & ACTIONS

*Gain lasting results from this conversation by asking yourself the following questions and noting your answers.*

## What is the meaning of this conversation?

## How can I apply this to my daily life?

## How can I do it successfully?

## What is the action being called for?

## What actions will I take?

## How can I apply this to my family?

# CONVERSATION #49

**BUT, WHAT ABOUT ME**
**WELL, IT'S NOT ABOUT YOU**
**IT'S ABOUT THEM**
*It's about what you have done*
*to trust them.*
*It's about what you have done*
*to inspire them.*
*It's about what you have done*
*to motivate them.*
*It's about what you have done*
*to respect them.*
*It's about what you have done*
*to value them.*
*It's about what you have done*
*to protect them.*
*It's about what you have done*
*to honor them.*
*It's about what you have done*
*to instruct them.*
*It's about what you have done*
*to involve them.*
*It's about what you have done*
*to enthuse them.*
*It's about what you have done*
*to encourage them.*
*It's about what you have done*
*to strengthen them.*
*It's about what you have done*
*to understand them.*
**WHEN IT'S ALL SAID AND DONE**
**IT'S ABOUT WHAT YOU DID FOR THEM**
**THEN AND ONLY THEN – WILL IT BE ABOUT YOU**

# THOUGHTS & ACTIONS

*Gain lasting results from this conversation by asking yourself the following questions and noting your answers.*

*What is the meaning of this conversation?*

*How can I apply this to my daily life?*

*How can I do it successfully?*

*What is the action being called for?*

*What actions will I take?*

*How can I apply this to my family?*

# CONVERSATION #50

## DIVIDE AND CONQUER

When problems begin to multiply,

divide and conquer one at a time.

Separate and place each problem

in a small box with a date for a

resolution written on the side

until there is nothing left to hide.

Close each and don't open until you

arrive at their target date for resolution.

Notice, that many will have been resolved or

diminished in their importance before they are opened.

For those that are left, set new dates until all are resolved or dissolved.

## WATCH YOUR PROBLEMS DISAPPEAR
## HIDING IN A BOX THAT'S BURIED NEAR

# THOUGHTS & ACTIONS

*Gain lasting results from this conversation by asking
yourself the following questions and noting your answers.*

### What is the meaning of this conversation?

### How can I apply this to my daily life?

### How can I do it successfully?

### What is the action being called for?

### What actions will I take?

### How can I apply this to my family?

# CONVERSATION #51

## BE LIKE AN ICEBERG

*When you're trying to impress, don't press,*

*just understate, listen closely and move slowly.*

*Leave most of what you know well below the surface.*

*Don't rush to tell them everything you know up front.*

*They just might think that's all there is.*

*Inject small hints about depth,*

*complexity and knowledge.*

*Be like an iceberg!*

*Let them imagine how*

*deep it really goes.*

## SAVE THE BEST FOR LAST

# THOUGHTS & ACTIONS

*Gain lasting results from this conversation by asking yourself the following questions and noting your answers.*

*What is the meaning of this conversation?*

*How can I apply this to my daily life?*

*How can I do it successfully?*

*What is the action being called for?*

*What actions will I take?*

*How can I apply this to my family?*

## CONVERSATION #52

### "HAVEN'T HAD SO MUCH FUN SINCE THE FLOOD"

*Say It with A Smile!*
*When confronted with*
*a negative experience, never*
*allow its perception to grow*
*beyond what it was meant to be.*
*Give it a humorous, light hearted,*
*comical twist to be saved and continually*
*repeated until all the negative feelings have*
*faded away. Do it and you will have magically*
*transformed that which was unbearable into*
*that which is now bearable.*
*It soon becomes the new*
*perception that quickly*
*transforms into*
*a new reality.*
*What happens*
*is not as important*
*as how you respond*
*to what happens to you.*

**SMILE AND THE WORLD SMILES WITH YOU**

# THOUGHTS & ACTIONS

*Gain lasting results from this conversation by asking
yourself the following questions and noting your answers.*

*What is the meaning of this conversation?*

*How can I apply this to my daily life?*

*How can I do it successfully?*

*What is the action being called for?*

*What actions will I take?*

*How can I apply this to my family?*

## CONVERSATION #53

### DISCOVER THE MAGIC

*If you stroll up and down the beach*

*you will come upon all types of people.*

*For those that you meet, look deep inside,*

*for what sets them apart from the rest.*

*Discover the magic they each possess and*

*you will soon find*

*you have gained*

*many close friends.*

**KEEP THIS UP AND YOU'LL END UP
HAVING A GREAT BEACH PARTY**

# THOUGHTS & ACTIONS

*Gain lasting results from this conversation by asking yourself the following questions and noting your answers.*

*What is the meaning of this conversation?*

*How can I apply this to my daily life?*

*How can I do it successfully?*

*What is the action being called for?*

*What actions will I take?*

*How can I apply this to my family?*

## CONVERSATION #54

*THOU SHALT NOT TAKE*
*WHAT IS NOT MINE*
*Never*

*downgrade*

*another life*

*to upgrade yours.*

*It has the opposite effect.*

*This transparent ploy instantly exposes*

*hidden insecurities one might possibly harbor.*

*Rather, project strong self-confidence by giving*

*unexpected praise, empathy and understanding.*

*BE ABOVE IT ALL*
*REAL CHARITY IS NOW DEDUCTIBLE*

# THOUGHTS & ACTIONS

*Gain lasting results from this conversation by asking yourself the following questions and noting your answers.*


*What is the meaning of this conversation?*


*How can I apply this to my daily life?*


*How can I do it successfully?*


*What is the action being called for?*


*What actions will I take?*


*How can I apply this to my family?*

# CONVERSATION #55

## A GIFT IS JUST A GIFT
*Never brag about
the gifts you received from The One up above
for a gift is still just a gift.*

*Never brag about
your looks, your brains or your athletic abilities
for they are still just gifts for you to embrace and enjoy.*

*Never brag about
those special gifts received
for they do not reflect upon what you have achieved.*

*Brag about
what you have achieved with the gifts you received,
like helping others climb the ladder of life.*

*Brag about
how you helped others
stifled some strife with the gifts you received.*

*Brag about
how you have made this place a better place
with those gifts received from The One up above.*

## OPEN YOUR GIFTS CAREFULLY
## USE EACH OF THEM WISELY
## GIVE THANKS FOR THEM PROFUSELY

# THOUGHTS & ACTIONS

*Gain lasting results from this conversation by asking yourself the following questions and noting your answers.*

### What is the meaning of this conversation?

### How can I apply this to my daily life?

### How can I do it successfully?

### What is the action being called for?

### What actions will I take?

### How can I apply this to my family?

# CONVERSATION #56

## THE SECRET FORMULA
*No one can take away what you have inside.*

*If you want to be more successful, work on what you have inside.*

*If you want to change your present, expand what you have inside.*

*If you want to improve your future, appreciate what you have inside.*

*If you want to experience more success, recognize what you have inside.*

*You already have all the ingredients for success inside.*

*All you need to do is believe in, work on and*

*improve what you already have - inside.*

## NOW THAT YOU HAVE THE INSIDE STORY
## JUST DO IT

# THOUGHTS & ACTIONS

*Gain lasting results from this conversation by asking
yourself the following questions and noting your answers.*

*What is the meaning of this conversation?*

*How can I apply this to my daily life?*

*How can I do it successfully?*

*What is the action being called for?*

*What actions will I take?*

*How can I apply this to my family?*

## CONVERSATION #57

### "PURE IMAGINATION"

*Imagine what would happen*

*if people listened intently to one another.*

*Imagine what would happen*

*if people discovered what others needed and delivered.*

*Imagine what would happen*

*if people listened with empathy and understanding.*

*Imagine what would happen*

*if everyone were given emotionally*

*what they needed most but could not ever find.*

*Imagine*

*what kind of world would we be living in.*

*What would it feel like?  What would it look like?*

*Imagine!*

*Anger would become a thing of the past.*

*Fear would be replaced with feelings of security.*

*Love would morph into a whole new meaning of trust and comfort.*

*Just maybe, bonded relationships would become the basis for personal success.*

### "COME WITH ME AND YOU'LL SOON BE
### IN A WORLD OF PURE IMAGINATION"

# THOUGHTS & ACTIONS

*Gain lasting results from this conversation by asking yourself the following questions and noting your answers.*

### What is the meaning of this conversation?

### How can I apply this to my daily life?

### How can I do it successfully?

### What is the action being called for?

### What actions will I take?

### How can I apply this to my family?

## CONVERSATION #58

### MODELING IS NOW IN VOGUE
Look for those who have attained great success.

Dig deep to find out their secret.

Precisely model what they do.

Copy how it all takes place

and you will become

a successful model.

### SMILE NICE
### FOR THE CAMERA

.

# THOUGHTS & ACTIONS

*Gain lasting results from this conversation by asking yourself the following questions and noting your answers.*

*What is the meaning of this conversation?*

*How can I apply this to my daily life?*

*How can I do it successfully?*

*What is the action being called for?*

*What actions will I take?*

*How can I apply this to my family?*

# CONVERSATION #59

## TRUST – THE GREATEST GIFT

*Trust has but one level. It's either there or it isn't.*

*Trust never comes in degrees or shades of gray. It is silent for it needs no announcement. It whispers acceptance for it needs no explanation.*

*It protects all relationships as it destroys potential conflicts.*

*It silently weaves a cherished bond between human beings.*

*It's easy to break but difficult to put back together.*

*It's never created with the words we speak.*

*It's the apex of confidence in another,*

*but only by the actions we take.*

*It's the highest attribute*

*of the human spirit.*

*It's the bedrock*

*of success.*

*Once you have it,*

*protect it,*

*embrace it*

*and enshrine it.*

*TRUST*
*KEEP IT IN A SAFE PLACE*

# THOUGHTS & ACTIONS

*Gain lasting results from this conversation by asking yourself the following questions and noting your answers.*


*What is the meaning of this conversation?*


*How can I apply this to my daily life?*


*How can I do it successfully?*


*What is the action being called for?*


*What actions will I take?*


*How can I apply this to my family?*

# CONVERSATION #60

## THE GREATEST MOTIVATOR

The higher your expectations, the higher will be your rewards.
High expectations become the great motivator in disguise,
in life, in sales and in your close relationships.
They operate in silence,
not from what you say,
but from what you don't say.
They come from what you silently expect,
for they are void of superfluous instructions
or meaningless evaluations.
They are crystalized in trust that
is given with a smile and
a nod of admiration.
They build confidence.
They improve lives.
They bind relationships.
They deliver positive results.
Expect trust and you will receive trust.
Expect pain and you will feel the pain.
Expect loyalty and you will receive loyalty.
Expect a cold and you will soon catch a cold.
Expect obedience and you'll receive obedience.
Expect failure and you will soon experience failure.
Expect agreement and you'll receive agreement.
Expect success and you will receive success.
The higher your expectations,
the higher your rewards.
The lower your expectations,
the lower will be your returns.
People live up to or down to your expectations.
Expect happiness and you will soon find happiness.
## BE CAREFUL OF YOUR EXPECTATIONS
## FOR THEY WILL SOON BE KNOCKING ON YOUR DOOR

# THOUGHTS & ACTIONS

*Gain lasting results from this conversation by asking yourself the following questions and noting your answers.*

### What is the meaning of this conversation?

### How can I apply this to my daily life?

### How can I do it successfully?

### What is the action being called for?

### What actions will I take?

### How can I apply this to my family?

# CONVERSATION #61

## PLAY THE GAME TO WIN
Life is a contact sport.
It is built upon body contact,
visual contact, emotional contact,
and precise mental contact. It is built
upon the communication of ideas,
feelings, needs, wants and emotions.
Make the right contact and you'll create
bonded connections. If you want to win
the game of life, learn how to communicate
with those with whom you are close and even
those who create moments of strife.

Assertive Communications is the game plan.
It just takes practice, repetition and perfection.
It's knowing when to speak, what to speak, how to speak and
controlling those messages sent without your intent.
Save yourself from serious penalties of the game
and keep everything moving to the goal line.
Today, you've got to play the game to win.

Here is a proven touchdown strategic play
you will discover from your answers to the following.
With whom do I want to communicate?
What do I want to say?
What do I want them to feel?
What do I want them to do?
When is the best time to do it?
How shall I communicate my message?
Practice this winning play until you have it perfected
and you will begin to experience what it feels like to win.
## NOW THAT YOU HAVE THE ANSWERS
## GET IN THE GAME TO WIN

# THOUGHTS & ACTIONS

*Gain lasting results from this conversation by asking yourself the following questions and noting your answers.*

*What is the meaning of this conversation?*

*How can I apply this to my daily life?*

*How can I do it successfully?*

*What is the action being called for?*

*What actions will I take?*

*How can I apply this to my family?*

# CONVERSATIONS #62

## CAREFULLY OPEN
## THE SECRET OF LIFE INSIDE
*It's Belief!*

*It's believing!*

*It's believing in yourself.*

*It's believing in The One up above.*

*It's believing in what you have inside.*

*It's believing you are here for a purpose.*

*It's believing in your capacity to enjoy life.*

*It's believing in the power of your mind.*

*It's believing in your ability to succeed.*

*It's believing in your dedication to learn.*

*It's believing in constant perseverance.*

*It's believing in your desire to help.*

*It's believing in your potential.*

*It's believing in your family.*

*It's believing in miracles.*

## NOW THAT YOU HAVE IT
## BELIEVE IT

# THOUGHTS & ACTIONS

*Gain lasting results from this conversation by asking yourself the following questions and noting your answers.*

What is the meaning of this conversation?

How can I apply this to my daily life?

How can I do it successfully?

What is the action being called for?

What actions will I take?

How can I apply this to my family?

# CONVERSATIONS #63

## HAVE YOU EVER BEEN TOUCHED?

*Have you ever been touched?*

*I mean really touched.*

*I don't mean physically.*

*I mean emotionally.*

*Plan now to touch.*

*Plan now to satisfy a need.*

*Plan now to ignite someone inside.*

*Plan now to make them feel different, happier*

*more confident, younger and more appreciated.*

*Do this and they will never, ever forget who you are.*

*Makes no difference if you are near or from afar,*

*they will find you, they will surround you*

*and they will royally crown you.*


*All behavior is motivated by unsatisfied needs.*

*It is the hot spot of life. Touch it and you will be astounded*

*by their response. Touch it and you will open all the gates inside.*

*Touch it and the music starts playing.*

*It's the key to the royal castle.*

### ENJOY YOUR REGAL RECEPTION

# THOUGHTS & ACTIONS

*Gain lasting results from this conversation by asking yourself the following questions and noting your answers.*

*What is the meaning of this conversation?*

*How can I apply this to my daily life?*

*How can I do it successfully?*

*What is the action being called for?*

*What actions will I take?*

*How can I apply this to my family?*

## CONVERSATION #64

*THE PRESENT IS NOW LEAVING THE STATION*
*The past is gone!*
*There is only this very minute.*
*The future has not arrived!*
*There is only*
*The Present!*
*What you do with the present*
*will affect how you move into the future.*
*Nothing is more important*
*than this very second,*
*this very moment,*
*this very minute.*
*Don't let another second go by*
*without giving it your close attention.*
*Good memories depend on how well you spend the present.*
*SURPRISE YOURSELF WITH A GREAT PRESENT TONIGHT*
*WRAP CAREFULLY*

# THOUGHTS & ACTIONS

*Gain lasting results from this conversation by asking yourself the following questions and noting your answers.*

*What is the meaning of this conversation?*

*How can I apply this to my daily life?*

*How can I do it successfully?*

*What is the action being called for?*

*What actions will I take?*

*How can I apply this to my family?*

# CONVERSATION #65

## EVERYONE HAS A STORY

If the truth be told
everyone has a story
that needs to be told.
It's not always pretty
and not always sad.
It's sometimes gritty
sometimes happy
but rarely mad.
If the truth be told,
it's not what you see on pulsating screens.
Like effervescent windows full of happy faces
just dancing their way through empty spaces,
giving an appearance life is only for the gifted
just for only those who show their social graces.
Soon we realize puckered lips and sparkling eyes
hide real-life tragedies never spoken,
speaking a strange language of coded lies,
for the many hearts that have been broken.
There is real life for those who have a story to tell.

Don't be fooled by what appears to be normal,
because the only normal is found in what is real.
Real life is a journey through the valley of heartbreaks,
walking through deserts of wants and sacrifices.
It's climbing majestic mountains just to be free
to breathe the rare air of pure happiness.
It's walking on the beach by the sea,
observing generations of waves,
erasing footprints in the sand.
For this is the story of life
and everyone has a story
to be told.

## IF YOU LISTEN TO THE STORY
## EACH HAS INSIDE
## YOU WILL SOON UNDERSTAND
## WHAT REAL LIFE IS MEANT TO BE

# THOUGHTS & ACTIONS

*Gain lasting results from this conversation by asking yourself the following questions and noting your answers.*

### What is the meaning of this conversation?

### How can I apply this to my daily life?

### How can I do it successfully?

### What is the action being called for?

### What actions will I take?

### How can I apply this to my family?

## CONVERSATION #66

### LIFE IS A JOURNEY

When you are about to plan your long journey in life, prepare properly.

Make sure you have a good map directing you to your destination.

Make sure you plan for alternate routes to where you want to go.

Make sure you learn much about where you are going.

Determine what you will need for the journey.

Don't ever look in the rear-view mirror.

That's the past and the future is now.

Leave markers. Light up your way.

Look ahead for what's ahead.

Plan for many obstacles.

Ask for help from The

One up above.

Learn from

those who

made the

journey

before.


### PREPARE

**AS IF YOUR LIFE
DEPENDED ON IT
ENJOY THE JOURNEY
IT'S THE TRIP OF A LIFETIME**

# THOUGHTS & ACTIONS

*Gain lasting results from this conversation by asking
yourself the following questions and noting your answers.*

*What is the meaning of this conversation?*

*How can I apply this to my daily life?*

*How can I do it successfully?*

*What is the action being called for?*

*What actions will I take?*

*How can I apply this to my family?*

## CONVERSATION #67

### YOU ARE NEVER ALONE

When you're feeling all alone,
when you feel completely lost in a crowd,
when your life is moving in the wrong direction,
when no one else seems to care about you

REMEMBER YOU ARE NEVER ALONE.

You have The One up above just waiting for your call.
You have The One up above always there by your side.
You have The One above who loves and cherishes you.
You have The One up above who created you.
Remember, He is there to help you be
what you were always meant to be.
All you must do is make the call.
Don't whisper and don't shout,
just have a quiet conversation
with The One up above.
Before you start,
open all your doors,
open all your windows.
Let The Light shine in
and enlighten you.
Let soft, warm
breezes
of inspiration
surround and
empower you.
Tell Him exactly how you feel.
Now take a deep breath, sit back and just listen!
ONCE YOU MAKE THE CALL
YOU'LL NEVER, EVER FEEL ALONE AGAIN

# CONCLUSION

We hope you have enjoyed all 67 conversation ideas, concepts and thoughts found inside. More than that, we hope they have given you a small degree of inspiration for a better way of communicating with yourself.
Our motivation is to help all of us enjoy
new possibilities by improving how we
talk to ourselves and in turn,
improving how we live.

Feel free to tell us your favorites.
Tell us the one that inspired you the most.
Tell us a positive result one of them delivered.
Tell us if any of them have changed your life
in some small way.

As we said in the very beginning,
happiness and success start on the inside.
How we talk to ourselves, inside,
is the difference between
success or failure.

We sincerely hope this provides you
something new to think about,
something interesting to talk about,
something challenging to act upon and
something exciting to do that will
change your life
forever.

Thank You,
Edward J. Peters
edpeters1@cox.net